Clinging to Bone

OTHER BOOKS BY
GARRY GOTTFRIEDSON

100 Years of Contact (1990)

In Honour of our Grandmothers (1994)

Glass Tepee (2002)

Painted Pony (2005)

Whiskey Bullets (2006)

Skin Like Mine (2010)

Jimmy Tames Horses (2012)

Chaos Inside Thunderstorms (2014)

Deaf Heaven (2016)

Clinging to Bone

GARRY GOTTFRIEDSON

RONSDALE

CLINGING TO BONE

RONSDALE PRESS
3350 West 21st Avenue, Vancouver, B.C., Canada V6S 1G7
www.ronsdalepress.com

Typesetting: Julie Cochrane, in New Baskerville 11 pt on 13.5
Cover Design: Julie Cochrane
Cover Art: Tania Willard
Paper: Enviro 100 Edition, 70 lb. Husky (FSC) — 100% post-consumer waste, totally chlorine-free and acid-free

Ronsdale Press wishes to thank the following for their support of its publishing program: the Canada Council for the Arts, the Government of Canada, the British Columbia Arts Council, and the Province of British Columbia through the Book Publishing Tax Credit Program.

Library and Archives Canada Cataloguing in Publication

Gottfriedson, Garry, 1954-, author
Clinging to bone / Garry Gottfriedson.

Poems.
Issued in print and electronic formats.
ISBN 978-1-55380-562-5 (softcover)
ISBN 978-1-55380-563-2 (ebook) / ISBN 978-1-55380-564-9 (pdf)

I. Title.

PS8563.O8388C55 2019 C811'.6 C2018-906386-6 C2018-906387-4

At Ronsdale Press we are committed to protecting the environment. To this end we are working with Canopy and printers to phase out our use of paper produced from ancient forests. This book is one step towards that goal.

Printed in Canada by Island Blue, Victoria, B.C.

for my brother,
Guy Duane Gottfriedson,
Cowboys and Indians
until our deaths

ACKNOWLEDGEMENTS

A special thanks goes out to Tania Willard, a wonderful Secwépemc artist who created the cover art for *Clinging to Bone*. I also want to acknowledge the great Tonga poet Karlo Mila for inspiring me to continue to write and see the world as it is, and for the hours we spend sharing our poetry from across oceans. And lastly, I want to thank my two closest friends, Jeff More and Louise Churisnoff, both for the time they gave listening to these poems and for their keen insights into my handling of sensitive issues.

CONTENTS

- Clear Memory -

- My Voice -

- Hunting Ground -

- This Holy Place -

This Holy Place

I was born with songs
surging from my throat
swirling in the blood of my life-givers
tossing in the currents
of trickster stories
of my Secwépemc ancestors

still fresh in my mind is
their last living image
standing on the shores of *setétkwe*
the river where my grandchildren now stand
humming songs to pull salmon from water to sky
tumbling in the waves at the banks and riverbeds of time

my long-gone relatives rattle
and drum small holy songs
atop the rippling river's waves
that lead to the lakes and headwaters
where the Salmon and Saskatoons
offer their spirits to us

we call this land Secwepemcúlucw

so powerful, so strong
they bend the ears of kindred spirits
filling hearts, our hearts
with courage to speak
for this land
for this water

for our future
for this holy place

Home

this is home
a protective place
where the naked self
escapes the prison
where the winds stop
beyond the walls outside
the place where dreams begin

this is home
where daylight enters
banishing grey shadows
bringing moments of enlightenment
warm and rare. enlightenment
charmed by dreamers
this is home

A Hunt of My Own

the stars bent down in autumn
blessing another generation
born in November's sharp air

my grandmother prepared
to imprint me
cleansed
my wet skin
caressing my naked body
with her touch
my nakedness bleeding
the charting of rivers
following the sound of a hunt
breaking silence

my father stood
at the river's edge
his soft heart mapping
tears along the riverbeds
returning with sage
and skin of *tśi7* — the deer
bundled into memory
for me to recognize
Secwepemcúlucw
its abundance
its beauty, like my matriarchs

(cont'd)

my father aching for me
to learn a hunt of my own
to smell *tśi7*
nestled in a bed
of dry leaves on an autumn floor
he humming land songs
into my baby soul
and whispering
"Secwépemc-ke!"
you are Secwépemc!
and I believed him
walking into my future

The Land's Skin

the frost thickens by night
seeping into earth by day

the land's skin makes ready
an armour for winter

heavy fog shields the sun by morning
lifts leaves to age by mid-day

transformation is difficult
but the skin sheds death

The Sap of Trees

in the sap of trees one senses
winter's restless purring for spring
seeping splendid soul songs
readying its blood beneath the skin
in a forest body aching release

ridges climb beyond the horizon
clothed in timber
the whistles of deer rutting
Píxenten — "the hunting place"
where the sap blood of pines and birch
long to open once more
to the sun's softening

this is the land of my ancestors
the hunters of life
Deer Dancing
the call of the wild
buckskin stitched by sinew
bound by pitch
quiver and bow
solemn in song
tromping down snow
anxious for the New Year Song
to bring all things alive once more

we are the gatherers of memory
recalling bone dust
layered inch by inch
it is the sound of plant shoots
breaking through to touch sky
offering sweetness to all things alive
it is the taste that lingers in the hunter's mouth
it is the colour of prayer
cupped in our humble hands
reaching beyond the horizon
tumbling back to the mountainsides
rolling into the rivers
calling on the salmon to fill our bellies
always remembering
who we are
our earthly brown skins
blending and bleeding into *Píxenten*
we are one with the land
we were born from it
our language arose deep from within
its belly rumbling sounds
that we use today
like trees in wind
our rough pelts smell of our birth
my birth — this earth

I am this land
I am the sap of trees
aching for release

Drifting

October mornings shimmer
glistening dew on red willow leaves
destined for death

magnificence is the sun's first rays
drifting over Secwepemcúlucw
to end another night of dreaming

stpútkwe7
"mist rises over water"
sprinkles splendour

chicadee sweeps
through the fir boughs
as the sun rises

so still is the mountain air
the breathing of water can be heard
by the Thunderbirds leaving

with each passing day
the skin of this land will tell
the story of burnt October

reminding the people
that this season, *sllwélsten,*
is an extension of eternal beauty

My Father

born Okanagan
with forgotten ties to Denmark
a mixed-blood like me
grew up too young
a man at fourteen
educated at St. George's
residential school in Lytton
a one-month dropout
he excommunicated Catholic schooling
to build a life on his own terms

Vernon

this is the place of my father's birth
I drive past his childhood home
where his footprints once marked
the weight of his life
my cousins call his home Dirty Lake
but how would I know its history?
my dad never spoke of his people

his spirit was beyond his years
for he joined my mother's tribe
as a young man of purpose
built a full life despite
the poison ivy strewn
along the Okanagan Trail
leading to Kamloops, my birthplace

so strange that I am a visitor here
misplaced by sprawling orchards
and vineyards marching up the hills
where they bow down to Okanagan Lake
its waves lapping against my feet
as I stumble along the shoreline
with my cousins nowhere near

Okanagan Valley

crow pierces the molten sky
eclipsing the citrus eye of noon
a flutter of wing dust spreads pockmarks
through August air in the Okanagan Valley

crow thinks only of flight and food
the bounty of roadkill picked bare
as the sun slants west
making room for a sunflower moon

golden delicious fields
disappear into a melting day
it is time to bed down for a night of dreaming
with the soft fluttering of black wings

breaking the silence of dusk
crow then sleeping until the moon
is swallowed by the morning sun
life once again renewed

Prince Albert

Prince Albert, Queen Victoria's beloved
sprawls over the prairie
along the banks of the North Saskatchewan River

gateway to the north
where red-haired Henry Kelsey
the first white to reach Saskatchewan
passed through with his Native guides
this place, a trading post, a mission,
the Cree named Kistahpinanihk
the "sitting pretty place"

but where did he sit, the young prince?
for he died
without ever touching this ground

Queen Street, Toronto

out with the old cold
and in with the new warm and fuzzy
urban rez cuzzies pan-handling
pan-Indian medicine-wheel love

all inclusive
all exclusive

Queen Street. insiders really rally
rez-zee outstanding
off-the-rez philosophy
white, black, red and yellow quarters

all inclusive
all exclusive

yet the mixed-blood reps rap foul
APTN style investigation
grind those hips, baby
Boyden is on the red carpet

all inclusive
all exclusive

Toronto tonto and blue-eyed Injun
spanking Boyden where they think it counts
but who's counting blood quantum anyway?
we were born with it all

all inclusive
all exclusive

Ottawa

the canal ice is a soft reminder
that this land is a place of movement
giving way to warmer days ahead
like warmth cupped in a lover's hands

within its crystals ice holds quiet beauty
offering joy even on the coldest days
and Ottawa has found her place in the cold
giving Canada its birthright

this city is alive with debate
voices from all nationalities
the gathering place where political will
rises and falls as days become centuries

beneath the Maple Leaf fluttering worldwide
the knowledge of First Nations peoples
almost escapes colonial memory
but as long as their names exist, so does this country

Yellowknife

in the land of the Inuit Sun
and Athabasca Moon
Yellowknife sits
amid diamonds

the soul of this land
and its people is rich
with acceptance
hearts open
beneath the northern lights
as they shimmer their way
towards midnight suns
discovering peace
and the promise that the world shines
long days of summer love

– Exhumation –

Ṫéẏ – The Women's Dance

this is *stseptékwll* — "the story"
of our mother's hands
gracefully twisting
a dance of appreciation
and the retelling of a million lives lived
like the leaf that flutters to earth
and has died many deaths
only to return to nurturing
like their hands
their hands fluttering
rebirth stories
bones upon bones
layers upon layers

it is *setsínem* — "their singing"
of snow-packed mountains
exploding ice as the earth thaws
under the weight of spring rain
bursting an abundance of new life
giving birth to the sound of returning thunder
an announcement of devotion
calling on the drums
singing deep throaty songs

this is *t̓éy̓* — "the women's dance"
butterfly floating over sweetgrass and moss
timber and lakes and rivers
hips telling the secrets of
bellies swelling, breasts full
delivering new layers of meaning
like water breaking
flowing and tumbling from caves
to breathe air for the first time
reaching back into the movement of women
our women, our women's hands cupping
tellqelmúcw — "those yet to be born"
hands dancing *stseptékwll* the one story
a million times more

Sanctified Brotherhood

this holy land does not create sins
religious men do

they keep secrets
hidden in rectums

hang rosaries above their beds
afraid the closet door will open

but when it does
a deal can be made

purity is the shaking of hands
around the boardroom table

all it takes is a pen sliding
across someone's future

the unity of the like-minded
fattens religious corporations

as they crawl out of sacred places
they shouldn't be in

Exhumation

it is time
to exhume
the stories from the grave
the journey of bones
grey and crumbling
clinging to souls
await the telling
of tribulations
of land stolen
sunny peaks
now luxury condos
children swallowed
and elders scorned
at the council tables
all in our language
Secwepemctsín
a language and a people
patient as the dust
they've become

Confusion

perhaps my poetry may entice
desire on sleepless nights
creating a mixed-blood
salad infusion
of saskatoons and eulachon

perhaps it is an expression
of the need to conquer
a sophisticated form of colonialism
a confused delusion of reconciliation
that terrifies and delights at once

perhaps this is why my poetry is
an arrow pointing at hearts
for those who are alive
remembering
the dead have yet to be heard

perhaps I am tired now
and have a headache
let me sleep

And Just Like That

and just like that,
it all comes out

beyond just a story, truth
deep down inside

the residential schools
their stories from survivors

the sun sees it all
surfacing

murdered and missing women
now driven by blood red songs

"reconciliation" so they call it
is not black and white words

skinning thin layers
off the tongue

reconciliation is admitting
prey was at stake

lives gunned down
in the name of church and crown

and just like that,
it all comes out

Foreigner

I have been a foreigner
in many places in this world
misplaced in the minds of others

my skin is the scent of Secwepemcúlucw
a rez Indian, a foreigner
in my own homeland

can you imagine that?

Earl's and the Rancher

it is spring in the north
calving season
nightshift for ranchers
sleep is for city folk
ranchers ridicule that
but know range-fed
cattle is a vogue

Earl's is a faithful patron
dishing out the perfect steak
a mosaic menu for a mosaic crowd
late evening delight timed perfectly
city folk schedule everything
plan out their lives an hour at a time
picky about what they eat
never dream of a rancher's life
yet pride themselves as
connoisseurs of dead cows

but back on the ranch,
cowboy nightshift may not
make the front page of
Better Homes and Gardens
and their fashion statement
may not include Dolce & Gabbana
but flip the page
from *Vogue* to the *Western Horsemen*
and you will see wranglers
and the Original Muck Boot Company
claiming prime place of page

so when the long sleep of winter thaws
a mingling of cow shit and mud
and the barnyard is a mess
and there is nothing pretty
about a prolapsed cervix
stuffed back and sewed up
remember who fills your belly

A New Year

they say
let the past go
black and clean

but it has
brought me this far
white survival

ahead of me
there is another
mile of silence

frozen in
last year's waste
as the snow falls in a new year

White Ascendancy

white ascendancy
white ascendancy
a mindset, the flow
of ink on paper
calligraphy centuries old
sculpting political policies

old words
old words
pink from tongues
hide the intent
break the hearts of warriors
crop the child at childhood

cripple
cripple
those who dare
to tromp down paths
leading old souls
to the apocalypse

kill
kill
those who poison salmon
and eat ceremoniously
while cynical leaders crawl out
to praise reconciliation

white is the new brown

Trends

self-loathing is growing
a cancerous cause of death
in Indian country

and tender offers and sunny ways
cannot wipe out the trauma
left over from the Indian Act

multiple lifetimes of death
greet our white brothers
what say you, Canada?

His Woman and a Nation

for Chief Wayne Christian

he weighs his woman down with his tears
anchoring her to the rocks in his heart
as if the burden of childbirth was not enough

he weighs his woman down with his tears
filling her heart with the crippling burden
that children are scooped into murky shadows

he weighs his woman down with his tears
as he struggles to see through the eyes of *sk'élep*
paths built by wine-drunk politicians and executives

he weighs his woman down with his tears
knowing the land issues are too complex
for one man to handle in a world gone wrong

he weighs his woman down with his tears
because she is a woman with the heart of her father
and she carries the nation he fights for

he weighs his woman down with his tears
because he is a man of his word
and he speaks with a loud voice

he weighs his woman down with his tears
fighting to protect the children he loves
because he was born with a father's heart

Democracy

this is the era of systematic mass incarceration
the American dream in the land of the free
the perpetuation of a different form of slavery
a money-making machine called "milk and honey"
death row politicians promising another great wall
wedged between Canada and Mexico
the "old ways" operate beneath scar tissue
do *black lives matter*?
people of colour buckled at their knees
children killed at the hands of the State
it is open season for police —
anytime, anywhere, anyway .

Standing Rock

the Standing Rock Sioux
with their song too near
sorrow's bones
the scent of death lingering
even as the heart of a nation
unwavering
declares a time of war

an oil pipeline
under the Missouri River
oil or clean water?
the harmony of night fades
even as Elder Allard
and her grandchildren
light a fire
in the brief dawn
of Standing Rock

standing up, unarmed warriors
proclaim anew
"we must kill the black snake"
and rename this world
for the love of the land

(cont'd)

“ReZpect our Water”
shout the young people
as they run protests
to Washington
that melt into song
music arising
out of a blanket covering
yesterday’s bones

but the company
holds the trump card
and so the black snake
continues its journey

Teníye

solitude
you own it,
old man moose

in Secwepemcúlucw
the weight of your bones
leaves imprints
your wild hair, a bushman's beard
a trademark for an open-sight gun
gun, a trigger
gun, a weapon
gun pointing at your heart, at your head
bowed above meadow grass
a lark chatters
the grass bends brown
sweaty palms,
an eye staring down the barrel
the discharge, the smell of gunpowder
and then the explosion
your last breath, a prayer

Clinging to Bone

Beautiful BC they called the magazine
this our land, Secwepemcúlucw
before the railroad came

with settlers in its wake
eating up the land
cutting down the forests

the huge pulp and paper mills
polluting the Thompson
dioxin and sulfuric acid

selling off our land
for sunny ski resorts
destroying the high alpine

—

now tree bark splits from inner ice
winter air stings against our skin
cells burn when exposed

trees bend
from the slightest wind
leak sap when thawing

earth awaits
new growth
as worms eat flesh

bring alive the unknown
skins shed
without us knowing it

snow falls
when it is summer
somewhere else

rain falls
when it is winter
somewhere else

—

movement is muscle memory
clinging to bone
fed by marrow

skeletons frame a song
worthy of praise
worthy of life

people sing
when faith is the only answer
we all sing

singing as Irene Billy
sang to Sun Peaks owners
Ohkudo Go Home

we need air
all things need air
clean air

clean cupboards
clean houses
clean this world

make room for shedding things
new skins
new insights

bring the land back
to its caregivers
the Secwépemc

A Cowboy History Lesson

beneath the redneck sun
the fat sky stretches
the blues in a northern hemisphere
the souls of mountains pegged
down with barbwire
post by post
strand by strand
bullet by bullet

cow punchers and calico queens staked
claims and cleaned out
this land of gold
that now remains for cows
eating roots to nothingness
scissor-sharp hooves slicing
anything indigenous to the land
reseeded with new infections

grazing ladies
giggling at
other mixed-blood cows
heads hung low
nibbling knapweed
and other imports
stuffed full in cat wagons
heading straight into round-up corrals

it's all worth tipping a hat
as the restless herd stirs
heavy heads bunked down
in buffalo-robe beds
skulls hanging from walls
broken feathers
broken hearts
stuffed in European pottery

vases gulch-dry tell the story
of how drought kills
but a corn juice nightcap tames
the jingle-jangles
a song does the trick, too
cowboy melodies woo
the choir mooing
as the night falls dark and cold

he dreams a new day, another chapter
acre-ocracy and barber's clerks
mouths full of corral dust
q-tips quivering in the ears
chapstick softening the lips
there is something to be heard
there is something to be spoken
survival or dominance

wild engines on the loose
range-riding bareback
all the while culling stock
branding irons in hand
heating up the rod
defining ownership
and identity — when it counts
important as the day's trendiness

who would not want to be a Marlboro man?
GQ slim with a fag drooping from his lips
Clint Eastwood eyes
shoulder drooping
under the weight of a saddle
an unbuttoned shirt
causing a trail of tears
a hunger worth crying

cowboys never get lost
in the winds of change
all things clear
this is the code
the cowboy code:
corral what belongs to you
never complain
never show pain

dance 'til the cows leave home
amid the dust aches and chaos
bringing on a city night
leaving a mark on history
like the dog that lifts its leg
and pisses on the territory
he claims
beneath the fat sky

Múlc

like the wet leaves of poplar shivering
drizzle, shaking off the blue
foreign eyes streaming fear,
we turned our backs
on all the dead white men
we buried in the sweetgrass smoke
expelled them all to their heaven

múlc — we named the poplar long before
the white man transformed himself to *Skalúla7*
the monster slicing Secwepemctsín from our holy tongues
when we swallowed the Queen's words
and she bled *múlc* from our throats and tongues
forgetting such words born from this land
forgetting their origins

instead, we watched the blue eyes of the whites
searching out the breasts of our women
who kept them alive, fed them, clothed them
nursed them back to tyranny
their ache for gold rotting their teeth
they divided the land into reservations
and broke the backs of Asians

their lust for a terra incognita
fouled the salmon rivers
brought in the mission men
forced our children
into residential schools
stripped the land of *múlc*
why did we not see it?

in the beginning, our wet and sticky eyes
were drawn to *múlc* singing
a melodic flutter awakening
the dance on forest floors, amid streams
trickling to rivers, and air, and sky
finally, returning home
for someone to remember you — *múlc*

your name, your sweet-scented body
your seeping sap nourishing
making medicine to keep
alive hearts barely beating
this word — your name
this tree — your love
wet and shivering has lived

even when wildfires raged
in the hearts of outlandish men
and our prayers, our feeble prayers
are heard by you, as we trek back
lie down beneath your soft tears
and thank you for our life-givers
forever more

- Clear Memory -

Eagle-horse Was Created in Haida Gwaii

for Robert Cross

there are many old souls
watching me through Robert's eyes

Raven eye-speaking to Eagle
two Haida camps — two Haida clans

I listen to spirit talk
as it builds on the ocean's waves

a primordial feast awaits
when the tide ebbs

it is an ancient roar
still relevant in our times

the slow sun will stretch
over a coloured western sky

and Robert will dream of the Eagle-horse
he will create this very night

its silver embodiment will be conceived
and ride my hand south tomorrow

it is a promise of Haida adoption in Haida Gwaii
a return to greet my brothers riding Eagle-horse

Clear Memory

the years whip
grey into the hair
oh so subtly

we have lived through
many storms
dreamed many nights away

time softened our hearts
brushed clear memory
out on the yellow canvas of sky

another night meant bones rested
another day meant life renewed
another year meant new stories

some things are meant
to be forgotten
but I remember all of you

Cohen's Poetry

Cohen's poetry
draws into itself
the sexual and mystical
knowing the world is broken
but celebrating
that very brokenness
"*Hallelujah,*" he shouts

but then warns
"*you want it darker*"
yet drawing on
the spice-box of earth
and the setting sun dissolving blue
the dying of longtime shining
the sky beginning at earth

a thought kindles
like stars against the sun
dreaming wide awake
of love's solitude
like grapes ready for wine
like a bird on the wire
like Cohen's poetry

Violet across the Sky

the sun streaks twilight haze
violet across the sky

a hummingbird in flight
wind whisks soft and swift

like words fluttering in my heart
wishing you were here

Growing Old

penmentsút-kuc — "find ourselves"
between the dead arms
of a tick, tick, ticking clock
dancing down seconds
black and white space
where numbers live
as bold as the passing years
we were baptized with time's weakness
twirling seconds to decades
so blessed were our lives
we had to ask ourselves
when does old age begin? or end?

I imagined us forever young
singing Indian love songs
reshaping a collection of dreams
fresh in our minds but weary of body
for we have seen many winters pass
telling it all as our wrinkled secrets
etched across our faces
some worthy of legend
others best left unsaid
like that moment before midnight
when my idle pleasures died
yet your eloquent reminders at dawn

(cont'd)

were more than one romantic reason
that brought us back to sing '49ers
at the Sarcee pow wow
harmonizing ageless love songs
together as we circle-danced
then played the *hand game*
these are the markers of our age,
our renewed blood
revitalizing our lives
we are everything beautiful in old age
finding ourselves late in life
when time has no pity

Landscapes

a cello of rain
strumming down
branch to branch
a pattern of notes
bending ears

listen closely

the rhythm of reincarnated souls
rebuilt from dust and wind-brushed
against rocks and bunch grass
create the progression
as sky brings renewed life

listen closely

the recognition of another
tied to the landscape of skin
bare memory
swelling tongues with love words
hearts open to music

listen closely

Moonlight at Harrison Hot Springs

moonlight shimmers
at Harrison Hot Springs
glimmering pathways
possibilities
sense is left
for daybreak

the sun sleeps the night away
heart's freedom full
fingers like butterflies
hovering searching
a spine glistening
beneath moon's rays

fire ignited
crackling
breaking rhythm
of the lakeside waves
lapping lapping
at the edge of lips

nothing exists
at this moment
but caressing bodies
purring softly
unfolding daybreak
at Harrison Hot Springs

New Moon

"soul's serenity"
I whispered

my arms around your waist
opening possibilities

the fire's song
crackling

sparks rise
searching heaven

skin against skin
the midnight breeze dawdles

sage and pine perfume
as your body sways

the blue night clinging
swinging below a new moon

flowers sleep
the night away

as we approached
soul's serenity

Jasper

I see the sad
maps in your eyes

you were born
in someone else's heart

and you wouldn't let me
trace the path

along your spine
my fingertips trembling

the throaty sound of crow
and rain drumming

swallows up the Rockies
rivers teeming in Jasper

I see your exit now
a turnoff near

they all have names
they are rich with names

offering obsidian love
in your curving path

melting into light
to find home

the fire is lit
and burns every memory

July Mornings in Tuscany

for Franco and Netta Bonfa

we no longer make love
as we did on July mornings
so many years ago

our lovemaking now is words
arguing in playful moments
in rooms full of tapestry

and as the evening sun drowns
the memories we speak of
over the passing years, we still live

as young lovers do on warm Tuscany nights
recalling our lives woven into sunsets
dreamers will never realize

so with each passing day, we know
our souls are bonded stronger
than the long days of July

Spider Solitaire

kings, queens and jacks
fingers crawling
caressing lingering
body scent addictions
to falling in love

helpless romantic jolts
heavy hearts cocooned
silky enchantments
of never-said-before
whisper puckers

the ace appearing
the game is addictive

Nearing Winter

when my eyes close at nightfall,
and the dusky blanket of dim night
shrouds my tired soul
I will reach deep into memory
reliving the love we offered
as a keepsake from the first time
we lay beneath the star-filled sky
nights and days not easily forgotten

I will time-travel backwards
to when your musky scent first engulfed me
a mixture of cedar and pine and juniper
at our first meeting amid the sagebrush
the time our grandmothers sent us out
to gather the sweetgrass
a smudge they offered as prayer
leading to the life we had in store

these days as I near the winter of my life
I yearn more and more to hear you, to smell you
and to swirl deep within you once again
I have never forgotten that morning we stood
in the early summer winds gathering prayers
fulfilling what our grandmothers
knew would grow — the celebration
they made for us is still alive

those sky-filled stars still sparkle
although my hair is now snow covered
my hands are river veins full of old blood
that ache to travel your petal-soft skin
I miss you still, I miss you still
I have lived for you, all of you
and when I close my eyes for the final time
will you come for me, my love, nearing winter?

- My Voice -

The Skies Bled Purple

my mother died
descending among teardrops
riding on the back of a swan
begging through song
to end the misery
of mourning souls

so strong were the lyrics
the skies bled purple
hearts at the graveside
and at the Feast for the Dead
legends began to unfold
as *sk'élep* appeared

and witness after witness
refused to forget
the matriarch solid as stone
beautiful as rain
dropping purple love
among the survivors

and like the greatest songs we know
she will be forever etched in memory

My Voice

for Violet

there will come a day
when my voice will not be heard

this body will fall
into a solemn hush

the scent of me will still be fresh
in the room where my last breath let go

the corridors of my house will be full
of my struggles for our language

the life I left behind
is the world I built for you

those who savoured my words
will know that regret is only a word

for life is about living
and death is perpetual silence

A Single Rose

I work silently
digging into myself
a pick and shovel in hand
the ground, cool,
like skin on a corpse

something has died
and I can see
the crows gathering
mourning their kin
speaking politely

your name drops
then spreads like water
the blue conversation
drowning out the sound
of rain filling the grave

the smell of the earth changes
as the mourners arrive
in solemn array to lay
bundles of dark flowers
I hold a single rose

Dark Mountains

in these days when the sun blinks
shadows along the mountainsides,
the long days of summer fade
into lengthening shadows

the scent of sorrow spreads
in the autumn air
early winter winds dizzy the heart
snowflakes melt on the tongue

the soul yearns to hear
summer storms smashing
rocks in a sea of sound
the body flush beneath layers

leaves curl crimson, burdened
heavy with the fall's deep mist
it is a poet's playground
a land full of metaphors

on the South Thompson
coyote and his son
turned into two boulders
for looking at naked girls bathing

see the boulders and learn to behave
the story tells us
the daring expression still ripe
the unexpected crispness in poetry

the stubborn will cling
to memories of spring
waiting for robin's return
to the shadowy masks of dark mountains

Daybreak

the autumn in me awaits
Artic winds sweeping south
promising the first brush of snow

violet skies burst
an array of hummingbird clouds
one thousand years of music in wind

my skin brittle with age
and I wonder
can you hear me break?

the winter in me awaits
the South Wind's rumbling thunder
stretching across snow-packed fields

to hold me in its embrace
as I wait for the ice-filled streams
of my chest to break free

take me into spring
I want to see
the gleam in your eyes at daybreak

Rumbles

I can hear my own voice
rumbling from a cave

fog now clouding
my once shining eyes

prophecy forever stilled
about our ancient pit houses

lost forever to development
on unceded land

not even valentine chocolates
and no more hands caressing soul

a boy-child in fetal position
smelling shame

what happened to the man?
not much of a man, he growls

Punching Bag

hanging

from the ceiling
        – a hook
        – a punching bag
        – a purple heart

dangled
battered

Hotel Monteleone, New Orleans

I wait watching
as Faulkner dawdles in these hallways

for there is nothing pretty
about whiskey drunks and stale beer
nothing macho
about hungry men talking dirty
choking back
chalk in the mouth
with a belly full of regrets
that a drunkard's sleep solves
on a New Orleans' eve
when through
the sound and the fury
Faulkner says it all

Clocks slay time . . .
time is dead as long as it is
being clicked off by little wheels;
only when the clock stops
does time come to life

a time never to come
and under the breath
a rose for Emily
who lived long and alone
a forgotten monument
regained by the pen
with a thin line
on yellow paper
tear-stained faded
on a *dry September night*
writing savagery

Faulkner, who lies dead
who writes from the place of death
gives me permission to dream lies
and dream, I do

The French Quarter

on Bourbon Street
even the deaf catch
the whisper of drunks
seeking stupefied sex
beer bottles slipping from sweaty hands
smashing love
out on the street
echoing off
smiling street merchants
auctioning merchandise

the night noise quickens, deep-fried
catfish are on display
sliding
all the way down,
the waiters are handsome
built a reputation
on the game
skilled and still smiling
tips 18 percent of the time
who would not pay?

this place is for falling
Cajun falling
Creole falling
deep-fried shrimp falling
love falling
southern flair
southern taste
black unsweetened ice tea
fills the void
if alcohol is not your thing

café conversation is light
Katrina is solid memory now
he says “look there”
points a manicured hand
beyond the air-conditioned
world to one of the fifty
breeches in the levees
visible still
and the wreckage of homes
no porches, no doors, no bedrooms

veterans’ fingertips sweep
the Iraqi war away
just outside the door
a clear view of night life
drops the nightmares
drops the drawers
male strippers belly dance
out on the street
bringing the night on
deep like the Mississippi

Capote became famous here
made up his own belly dance
working *in cold blood*
for his own fortune
Faulkner lived in Pirate’s Alley
wrote his satire
on the 1920’s literary scene
delved into the city’s corners
everywhere
there is sexy

sexy teeth
sexy treats
sexy tits
sexy sounds
sexy snapshots
sexy images
inked along the arms,
around the neck
all the way down
to deep southern warmth

Tennessee Williams wrote of glass
telling Laura *to blow*
out her candles
for *the world is lit by lightning*
Hemingway was brilliant
at 214 Royal Street
with his *night before battle*
lapping up the sweat
and three-for-one beer
so the beat goes on

fall to your knees, baby
French style
campy as hell
the French Quarter never sleeps
Rue Bourbon still
has eyes wide open
owls don't blink
says Gardner
the iPhone in the bedrooms
catching it all

Barcelona

the wind forever blows
in the streets of Barcelona

the Mediterranean's hot breath plays
off the beaches where ghosts drown

among the cerveza drunks
where Columbus is forgotten

this city cries its age
worn down on cobblestone streets

and buildings blasted
in the civil war, a world war

where El Caudillo broke the republic
leaving Catalonia to cry for its soul

the sand grinds secrets here
whispering in Catalan syllables

these steamy streets are weighed down
with dead monarchs and a passion for living

yet, the churches are full of bloody gold
reminders of ancient wrongs in the new world

in this modern age, the tapas bars natter but
the city's history is kept alive only in museums

today, I walk over each echoing cobblestone
trying to find the winds to take me home

Barcelona, I am dying of thirst

Vienna

I turned my heart
around to seek
Mozart beauty
amid despised refugees
graffiti-filled streets and
cracking sidewalks
cupping dandelions

there are no other flowers here
just the grey smell of disappointment
among the bomb-beaten buildings
lingering in the scent of invasions
I imagined it wasn't always this way
with Beethoven and Sigmund Freud
wandering in the Schönbrunn gardens

Vienna, how you sadden
the spirits of lovers
spreading sorrow
within remnants of Nazi desire
pulsing in the underworld
fighting another kind
of survival recalling the *Anschluss*

with cheering Austrians welcoming
their beloved son, Adolph Hitler
there is no splendour
in dead men walking
the Hapsburgs have not died
roaming among dead loved ones
wrapped in barbwire at Albertinaplatz

the Monument Against War and Fascism
remembers the victims of war
chained slave labourers, a dying woman
all reminding the Austrian pride
that wars make history
that lust is instinctive
that betrayal has a price

no one will remember
me in history
I fought in no war
did not betray my people
but I shudder just the same
turn my heart away
write this memory of you

I say to you — Vienna
farewell forever more
no more Opera House
no more Sachertorte
I am flying home
my heart full of Mozart
never to return to you

- Hunting Ground -

Like Moon and His Four Wives

like Moon and his four wives
they were all prisoners
in a cave of icicles
dripping from the sunset sky
teasing his heart
melting their bones
drop by drop

in a cave crying ice,
he listened to the Eagles
on nights of dry love,
humming the lyrics to another
tequila sunrise cocktail
knowing regret was a toy
he played with
a song he remembered well

xpiqtsín — "the thin white lips of morning" arose
whispered hungry words
cmuqwtsentséms
the ghosts of his wives "stuffed his mouth full
of something" he could not handle
wild rose pedals they fed him
until he choked on his tongue
like a passed-out drunk
dying in his own dreams

like Moon and his four wives

Hunting Ground

I have seen
him cry
grown man tears
heartsick waiting
to see through
the eyes of *sk'élep*
a new home
for a green people

his sorrow kept
alive by broken treaties
stolen land
languages lost
that break hearts
and starve souls
making his ancestors
ghosts

The Chopped Leaf Café

I watch young lovers
across the room
at The Chopped Leaf café
phones at the ready
giggling silly eye to eye
with mischievous hungers

far from understanding
that to be in love never lasts
relentless though it may be
they nibble on cannabis buds
savour the salt of black olives
their tongues roving

eager to try it all
eager to go down
eager to take a chance
so young in love
unafraid of waywardness
who could imagine that?

Last Night

I looked the man in the eye
a hand swiping at blurred lines
in a steamed-over mirror
after an early morning shower
an overnight stranger appears
staring back zoning in
on the ruffled sheets
the clothes strewn across the cold floor
for the fire went out
last night

Husbands & Wives

a bull is always
best left for pasture breeding

their balls drag the ground
until they are kicked back into shape

the electric fence around the yard
keeps a husband at home

but poking the head under the wire
in search of a full belly

doesn't mean finding
a table full of grub

there is nothing greener
than what grows at home

and there is no need for a nose ring
unless escape is the only option

Risks

the saucer-eyed boy throbs
anticipation
a mischievous night out
pepper singeing his groin
slicked-back hair
Elvis Presley style
shiny for the taking

it's a young man's dream
to introduce his
macho manoeuvres
but troubled
that he might drown
if his trendy night moves
cause snickering smiles

yet there remains
an edge of excitement
when he sees the possibilities
of lonely gals with swivelling hips
then he remembers
cougars have sharp eyes
glowing in dark places

they have flesh-wounding claws
able to rake the backs of forests
and tongues purring seduction —
but knowing the forest well
that it is a playground
a classroom of sexual etiquette
for those who dare

pencil in mind, taking careful notes
he watches her
set claim to her dance-floor
laboratory, music booming
pulsing lessons to be learned
when she draws the map
the comfort inn a mile away

floating between the space of hearts
she skillfully lures him
into the cougar cave
unbuttons his 501s
down on her knees
it is all about transformation
the unknown becoming the known

the risks are worth it
or so he thinks
as he closes his eyes
rocks back to the bed
the two of them
devoured and devouring
deep in the cougar cave

Horse Dancers

some men were born dancers
slow getting dressed
slow getting undressed

the touch of tongues
thunder drums
shaking the night
warm winds whispering
along the back of a neck
down to the belly
into the underworld

lightning strikes sorrel horses
fancy and eager
to rove dancing
parting grass
bending wind
slow and gentle
primitive rumbles
enticing whimsical sound
rhythms and knowing
and then the release

A Cruel Affair

affairs are deadly acts
flowers without water
an aching thirst
faint words
clinging onto life
hopeless prayers
and stale kisses
the perfume
of goodbye is genuine
fresh on the suitcase handle
walking into disappearance
and there is no turning back

divorce is a cruel affair

Beer Bath

self-sabotage is an addiction
drowning in a beer bath
seeing Kitty Wells' ghost
singing *it wasn't God*
who made
honky tonk angels

there he is
slumped on a bar stool
shadow dancing
bellies full of gloating rights
yet paying once again
for that *back street affair*

addicts are experts of exclusion
singing songs for drunken ghosts
dropping to their knees
carving the sign of the cross
into bony chests
bleeding atheist prayers

there is no honey left
remembering the sad lyrics
of lost country girls
on the lonely side of town
none of it makes sense
in *Heartbreak U.S.A*

Graves

standing at the graveyard
a magpie chatters in black and white

for the children of St. Joseph's
buried here unattended

rain will nurture the land tomorrow
and more violets will grow in the days to come

but the parents will continue
to carry the heavy casket of the mind

The Empty Belly of Wind

there are no more
heroes or martyrs left

the world is drunk
on torrid romance

the slavery of big businesses
brings cynicism to the surface

saintly men — soft devils
sporting erections over bibles

the deal is done
the hero's grip slips

—

the Pope guarantees heaven
but heaven is sold

corporations buy and build fat empires
and monarchs are useless entities

sport killing is the game
currency is the rule

there are no more
heroes or martyrs left

—

the broken-winged sparrows
are lost in soundless flight

surviving starvation
in the empty belly of wind

there is a hole in the sky
the sun is disoriented

all things die screaming
even the genius of man

Winter Is Gone

all night the wind shouted at the lake
tumbling tears wore away the edge
rattling nonsense-whipping words
into blizzards of atonement

"I release you,
I release you at the threshold
I relinquish my life for yours"
the wind murmured

a time to raise our eyes
a time for winter prayers
clouds gathered at the wind's will
softening violent voices

a message clear
left for the living
awaiting spring to fall upon the land
blooming once more a welcome

dissolving winter's sorrow
among sleeping trees
scrolling words of peace for us
winter is gone

SECWÉPEMC GLOSSARY

cmuqwtsentséms: they stuffed my mouth full of something
Kistahpinanihk (Cree): the sitting pretty place
múlc: poplar tree
penmentsút-kuc: find ourselves
Píxenten: the hunting place
Secwépemc: Shuswap People
Secwepemctsín: Shuswap language
Secwepemcúlucw: Land of the Shuswap
setétkwe: the river
setsínem: their singing
Skalúla7: childhood monster
sk'élep: coyote
sllwélsten: autumn
stpút̓kwe7: mist rising over the waters
stseptékwll: creation stories
tellqelmúcw: those yet to be born
teníye: moose
t̓éy̓: the women's dance
Tk'emlups: Kamloops
tśi7: deer
xpiqtsín: white thin line of the sky in early morning

ABOUT THE AUTHOR

Garry Gottfriedson, from the Secwépemc nation (Shuswap), was born, raised and lives in Kamloops, British Columbia. Growing up on a ranch in a ranching and rodeo family, he has been fully immersed in his people's traditions and spirituality. He comes from four generations of horse people. His passion for horses, raising and training them, still continues to this day. He holds a Master of Education from Simon Fraser University, and he has studied Creative Writing at the Naropa Institute in Boulder, Colorado. For a number of years he was a teacher and school principal. His published works include *100 Years of Contact* (SCES, 1990); *In Honour of Our Grandmothers* (Theytus, 1994); *Glass Tepee* (Thistledown, 2002, and nominated for First People's Publishing Award, 2004); *Painted Pony* (Partners in Publishing, 2005); *Whiskey Bullets* (Ronsdale, 2006, and Anskohk Aboriginal Award finalist); *Skin Like Mine* (Ronsdale, 2010, and shortlisted for Canadian Authors Association Award for Poetry); *Jimmy Tames Horses* (Kegedonce, 2012); *Chaos Inside Thunderstorms* (Ronsdale, 2014); and *Deaf Heaven* (Ronsdale, 2016). His works have been anthologized both nationally and internationally. He has read from his work across Canada, in the USA, Europe, Asia and only recently returned from a reading tour throughout New Zealand.